the COLLECT[...]

Hawthorn

SAGE PRESS

Published in 2001

SAGE PRESS,

PO Box Nº 1, Rye, East Sussex TN36 6HN.
e-mail: sagepress.bm@btinternet.com
www.sagepress.co.uk
Sage Press 2001

All rights reserved.

Set in Palatine italic 9 on 11 point leading.
Display in Palatino Light Italic 48 point.

Design and Illustrations
Chris Monk of Yellowduck Design & Illustration.

Research & Text
Cindy Stevens

Series Editor and Publisher
Mrs Bobby Meyer

Printed by M & W Morgan Printers, Hastings

This book is sold subject to the condition
that it shall not, by way of trade or otherwise,
be lent, re-sold, hired out, or otherwise circulated
without the publisher's prior consent in any form
of binding or cover other than in which it is
published and without a similar condition
including this condition being
imposed on the subsequent purchaser.

ISBN: 0 - 9531644 – 8 – 9

Hawthorn

'And every shepherd tells his tale
'Under the hawthorn in the dale.'
                    (Milton, L'Allegro)

The hawthorn is probably the commonest hedgerow tree in Britain, and its importance is reflected both in the number of places to which it has given its name and in the great variety of local names which it possesses.

Commonly used names are whitethorn, quickset (or quickthorn) and may, but it has been called many others, ranging from moonflower and holy innocents to the more prosaic tramp's supper.

There are many literary references to hawthorns and it has an important place in legend. Its medicinal uses are many and various, and there is much folk tradition associated with the tree.

Hawthorn has long been used as a boundary marker and is a valuable host for wildlife. Its blossom is a wonderful sight.

'The risen cream of all the milkiness of May-time.'
                    (H.E. Bates).

Hawthorn in legend and tradition

The Glastonbury Thorn

Probably the most famous legend associated with the hawthorn is that concerning Joseph of Arimathea who, fleeing from persecution, returned to his old haunts in south-western England (he had apparently been a Phoenician tin-trader). In one version, he planted his staff of hawthorn on a hill near Glastonbury; in another, he brought with him part of the Crown of Thorns. In both cases, the plant grew very quickly and flowered on old Christmas Day (early January). Joseph celebrated this miracle by building the first church in England, St. Mary's, at Glastonbury. The tree's second flowering, at Easter, is said to continue the symbolism of Christ's birth and resurrection.

The connection with Joseph of Arimathea was not made in print until the seventeenth century although the tradition was already strong by then. The Puritans considered any ceremony concerning the Thorn to be idolatrous and had what was believed to be the original tree destroyed. However, so many cuttings had been taken from it over the years that it was easily replaced. Its alleged descendants are to be found in many parts of the country, flowering twice a year and sometimes remaining evergreen.

'Thre hawthornes also, that groweth in Werale (Weary-All Hill near Glastonbury),

'Do burge and bere grene leaves at Christmas
'As freshe as other in May when ye nightingale

'Wrestes out her notes musycall as pure glas.'
(Anon., early 17th century).

A sprig from the tree at St John's Church, Glastonbury, is still sent to the reigning monarch every Christmas. The 'original' tree, whose stump is recorded as having still been in existence until 1750, had its site marked in 1800: J A anno d.XXXI. Apparently, it had had two trunks until the time of Elizabeth I, when one was destroyed by a vandal. The perpetrator of this act subsequently lost both an eye and a leg, in accidents which were no doubt seen as just retribution.

Some of the descendants of the Glastonbury Tree also had ceremonies attached to them. That at Appleton, in Cheshire – 'bawming the thorn' – involved dressing the tree with red ribbons and flags, to commemorate its planting by Adam de Dutton on his return from the Crusades in 1125. It took place at midsummer but became too rowdy and so was suppressed by the Victorians.

Hawthorn has been revered as sacred, both for Christians – because of its traditional association with the Crown of Thorns – and in other cultures. There is an ancient myth that it sprang from the place where lightning hit the earth. The ancient Greeks saw it as an emblem of hope and good augury. It has been known as a love amulet and a protector from evil since at least the first century BC, especially in England and France. Through the ages it has for some been a symbol of marriage and fertility.

In Ireland it is said that a hawthorn tree growing in the middle of a country road will always be left standing regardless of traffic. Still in Ireland hawthorn has been linked with the saints or called the 'mass-tree', often being a resting-place for coffin-bearers and sometimes associated with the 'little people', marking their meeting-places close to burial mounds. In Britain, too, there is a fairy link: old trees standing alone may be fairy meeting-places.

Hawthorn flowers were believed to carry the smell of the Great Plague of London – some saying a smell of carrion – and indeed records show an increase in number after the Black Death. There is some factual basis for these beliefs, as well as for the apparently contradictory trust in the healing properties of this tree.

There is even a somewhat morbid myth that hawthorn flowers were used for the wreaths worn by human sacrifices at Celtic spring festivals.

Hawthorn is associated with the Virgin Mary, and May altars used to be made to her in both churches and homes. In England, these were banned after the Reformation, but the link with Roman Catholicism remained. Apparently, recusant Catholics would put a sprig of hawthorn in a window to show others that a priest would be saying Mass there. However, it has also been suggested that the link between the Virgin and hawthorn did not appear until the eighteenth century, in Italy.

There are many folk traditions resulting from these beliefs. In some parts of the country, it was considered dangerous to take anything from an isolated 'fairy thorn'.

According to the Scottish Statistical Report of 1796, there was a hawthorn in one area '… for which the people have a superstitious veneration. They have a mortal dread to lop off or cut any part of it, and affirm with a religious horror that some persons who had the temerity to hurt it were afterwards severely punished for their sacrilege.'

There was thought to be some risk of fairy enchantment associated with the tree and it was considered inadvisable to sit under a hawthorn on May Day, Midsummer's Eve and Hallowe'en. Apparently, these were the only days on which the fairies would cast spells upon humans. Certainly, the welcome shade of hawthorns is often referred to in literature.

Hawthorn as protector

Hawthorn has been seen as both a protector and a threat. Hawthorn twigs were hung over babies' cradles for protection against ill, but the blossom itself was considered dangerous. In some areas, bringing the flowers into a house foretold the death of a family member; in others, it was a harbinger of more general bad luck. It was especially disastrous to sleep in a room with hawthorn blossom. In Wales, there was a belief that bringing the flowers into the house would cause the death of the mother: the name for the hawthorn, blodau marw mam, *literally means flowers-die-mother.*

Hawthorn was seen as a specific protector against lightning:

> 'Creep under the thorn
> It will save you from harm.'

Since there was a belief that the Crown of Thorns was made from hawthorn and that lightning was the work of the devil, tradition had it that lightning could not strike a plant that had touched Christ's brow.

The tradition of bringing hawthorn into the house on Maundy Thursday, and keeping it there as a lightning protector, was said to be effective because

> *'Under a thorn*
> *'Our Saviour was born'.*

May Day

By far the most important tradition associated with hawthorn is May Day with its attendant sexual licence. The maypole, a phallic symbol of rebirth, was frequently made of hawthorn, although beech and oak were also used. Sprays of hawthorn were made into garlands and other decorations. Another ancient traditional symbol heralding returning summer is the Green Man, frequently depicted as carvings in ancient buildings and churches and often shown with a wreath of hawthorn entwined around his head and sometimes sprouting out of his mouth.

Going a-maying was a popular English spring ritual when sprays of blossoming hawthorn were brought home with due ceremony. After the reform of the calendar, however, many other spring flowers and greenery were substituted since the hawthorn was more rarely in bloom by the new 1st May.

This particular ritual is known not to have been the preserve of the country folk alone: King Henry VIII is reported as going a-maying from Greenwich to Shooter's Hill "with his Queen Katherine, accompanied by many lords and ladies."

The sprays were used to decorate the outside of houses but were not brought inside (other than into churches) because of the belief that it was a harbinger of death.

A number of traditional maying songs survive, from different parts of the country. They were sung in house-to-house processions when a ceremonial wreath of hawthorn and flowers was exhibited or sprays of hawthorn used to decorate each house.

One verse of the Peterborough song gives a taste of the ceremony:

> 'This bunch of May it looks so gay,
> 'Before your door it stands;
> 'It is but a sprout but it's well spread out
> 'By the work of our Lord's Hands.'

In some parts of the country, washing in hawthorn dew was thought to bring beauty:

> 'The fair maid who the first of May
> 'Goes to the field at break of day
> 'And washes in dew from the hawthorn tree
> 'Will ever after handsome be.'

In Suffolk, the first person to find a hawthorn branch in full blossom on May Day would be rewarded with a dish of cream.

The ritual of may birching was carried out in some areas until the late nineteenth century. Late on May Eve, the birchers would leave sprays of plants in the doorways of houses, each plant carefully chosen to show the virtues or vices of the occupants.

Flowering hawthorn was seen as a compliment, while any other thorn meant quite the reverse.

May Day was often used as an excuse for sexual licence. Writing in 1583, Philip Stubbes described his horror at the practice of maying: 'I have heard it credibly reported...that of forty, or a hundred maids going to the wood..., there have scarcely the third part of them returned home undefiled.' (Anatomie of Abuses). And many Maying songs have double-entendres in them.

'In contrast to Christmastide greenery and Easter willow, (hawthorn) is a plant kept outdoors, associated with unregulated love in the fields rather than conjugal love in the bed" (the anthropologist Jack Goody).

The links with fertility were also important in earlier times. The ancient Greeks carried hawthorn at weddings, while a Roman bridegroom would wave a sprig as he went to his nuptial bed in a room lit by torches of hawthorn.

Hawthorn as a boundary

Hawthorn has frequently been used as a boundary marker or landmark tree. A survey of 878 Anglo-Saxon records found that 38.7% of individually named trees were hawthorn. The next most common tree, oak, represented only 13.1% of the total. However, this could be due simply to the fact that these records were accounts of walks, or beatings of bounds, which generally took place at the Christian Festival of Rogationtide when the hawthorn was likely to be in full flower and so particularly noticeable.

Some hawthorn markers are very old. One at Salcombe Regis in Devon carries the following inscription: 'A thorn tree has been maintained here since Saxon times when it marked the boundary between the cultivated field of the coombe and the open common of the hill.' The Hethel Old Thorn, or Witch of Hethel, in Norfolk, which has long served as both boundary marker and meeting place, is believed to be more than 700 years old. It was mentioned in a thirteenth century charter, and the fact that its girth was over twenty feet (six metres) in the mid-eighteenth century suggests that it is indeed the original.

Scotland, too, has its notable hawthorns. One near Kilmeford in Argyll was used as a wishing tree, having coins hammered into it. And, more curiously, at Selkirk in 1811, it was used as a boundary marker for French prisoners of war who were allowed to take exercise by walking the two miles to 'the Prisoners' bush', a single hawthorn.

Hawthorn was often coppiced or pollarded: some in Hatfield Forest are fifty feet (fifteen metres) high with trunks of three to four feet (one metre) in circumference.

Hawthorn spinnies, which are self-perpetuating, can last for a very long time. One on Goonhilly Down in Cornwall is mentioned in records of 977 AD.

Hedgerows

Hawthorn is probably the most common hedgerow tree in Britain. Because it grows rapidly, giving rise to the names quickset or quickthorn, it was much used following the Enclosures Act in England: 'plots of land allotted by virtue of this Act shall be enclosed and fenced around with ditches and quickset hedges.' During the eighteenth and nineteenth centuries, some 200 000 miles of hawthorn hedge were planted. Sadly, the latter part of the twentieth century has seen the loss of many of these hedges, to make allowance for the size of new farming machinery or to save the cost of labour keeping them trimmed.

Hawthorn hedges give good protection to birds because they are so dense and early to leaf. A fascinating study proves this, showing that in 1967 an average of 34 pairs of birds, of 19 different species were found per 1 000 yards of dense, overgrown hedge.

Hawthorn is occasionally used in topiary, most frequently being trimmed into balls or bird shapes. Its hedges are sometimes trimmed for specific purposes such as spreading laundry to dry. More comically, in the Isle of Man milk pails were hung to dry from hawthorn hedges.

Hawthorn is often a host for mistletoe. A survey carried out in Shropshire in the 1980s found 22% of trees bearing the plant to be hawthorn. Mistletoe has even been reported growing on hawthorns on a steep mountainside in Wales.

Place names

Because it is so widespread, growing under a variety of conditions and even tolerating deep shade, hawthorn has given its name to many places. Some have the word 'thorn' in their name: Copthorne, Thorney Island, Thornhill, Thornton and many others. The word 'hay' also comes from the tree: Haywards Heath, Hayes and Hay-on-Wye are just a few examples. Many of these places will be on chalk, where hawthorn is particularly prominent.

Local names for hawthorn

Being such a common tree, hawthorn has acquired many different local names. Some, like the widely used quickset *and* whitethorn, *refer to its physical characteristics: in these cases, the speed of growth and colour of its wood. Others, such as* holy innocents, *show its mystical connections. Yet others are more practical: the names* tramp's supper *and* bread and cheese *presumably refer to the edible nature of various parts of the tree. A local Sussex hedgelayer recalls eating hawthorn leaves as a child and finding them most tasty.*

There are also many different names for the berries, reflecting their use as food for various species: bird's meat, chucky cheese, pig-berry *and* pixie pear *are but a few.*

Weather lore

The familiar saying 'Ne'er cast a clout 'til May is out' almost certainly refers to the tree rather than the month.

Early blossom indicates a premature 'false' spring
    'When the hawthorn bloom too early shows
    'We shall have still many snows.'

And, like the holly, too many berries are a bad augury
    'Many haws, many sloes,
    'Many cold toes.'

The uses of hawthorn

Medicinal

Hawthorn has long been used for medicinal purposes. It is widely used in cases of hypertension, to steady the heartbeat and to increase oxygen levels to the heart. It has also been recommended for conditions as diverse as gout, pleurisy, vertigo, haemorrhage and insomnia.

A decoction from the bark is used to reduce fever. Its berries are considered effective against diarrhoea, and are used in Russia in cases of amoebic dysentery.

An infusion of the berries makes a good gargle for sore throats and a decoction of the flowers and berries is said to be a good remedy for skin problems.

The old herbalists recommended the use of distilled water made from the haws (fruit) to remove splinters. Culpeper, writing in the seventeenth century, said that, applied to 'any place where thorns and splinters doe abide in the flesh (it would) notably draw them out…thus you see the thorn gives a medicine for its own pricking…'.

Culpeper also recommended taking the powdered seeds in wine as a treatment for dropsy, and bruised seeds boiled in wine for "inward tormenting pains".

Food

It is not commonly known today that the fruit of the hawthorn can be used for making preserves and a particularly good jelly when cooked with crab-apples, which serve to provide the necessary pectin. They can also be made into a brandy-based liqueur. When eaten raw the berries are said to taste like sweet potato.

The leaves can be used in a variety of ways. In the past, they were chewed simply to appease hunger; but recently some adventurous cooks have experimented and say that the nutty tasting young leaves in April make a good addition to salads. They can also be added to cheese on toast or used with bacon to make a savoury roll.

Some recipes

Hawthorn flower liqueur: fill a wide-necked bottle with the flowers, with their stalks removed, sprinkle with sugar (two tablespoonsful for an average-sized bottle), cover with brandy. Keep for at least three months, shaking occasionally. Strain and seal, it is now ready to drink.

Savoury roll: roll out some suet pastry, cover with young hawthorn leaves and strips of bacon, season and roll up. Steam in a cloth for at least an hour. Serve sliced with gravy.

Hawthorn provides food for wildlife. Bank voles eat the fleshy part of the haws or berries, as do many birds. Blackbirds and mistle-thrushes are particularly fond of them.

Greenfinches, with their broad, heavy beaks acting as nutcrackers, prefer the seeds in the middle of the haws.

Wood

The wood of the hawthorn is hard and durable. Its most common uses in the past were for handles, rake tines and similar practical objects. It has also been used for printing blocks.

The root wood, which is fine-grained and polishes very well, has been used to make small items such as combs and boxes.

Hawthorn is the hottest wood for burning. It is claimed that charcoal made from the wood can melt pig-iron without the aid of a blast.

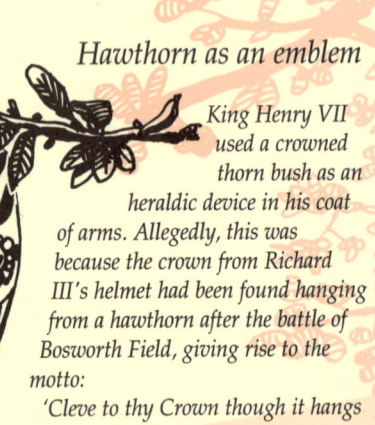

Hawthorn as an emblem

King Henry VII used a crowned thorn bush as an heraldic device in his coat of arms. Allegedly, this was because the crown from Richard III's helmet had been found hanging from a hawthorn after the battle of Bosworth Field, giving rise to the motto:

'Cleve to thy Crown though it hangs on a bush.'

Hawthorn in literature

Shakespeare makes references to hawthorn, although he does not share the belief that Richard III's crown was found on a bush.

He refers to its shade:
>'Gives not the hawthorn bush a sweeter shade
>'To shepherds, looking on their silly sheep,
>'Than doth a rich embroidered canopy
>'To kings that fear their subjects' treachery?'
>
>(Henry VI Part 3)

And to its shelter:
>'This green plot shall be our stage,
>'This hawthorn brake our tiring-house.'
>
>(A Midsummer Night's Dream)

In The Idylls of the King, *Tennyson says:*
>'Blow trumpet, for the world is white with May.'
>
>(The Coming of King Arthur)

And Robert Burns, in his Lament for Mary, Queen of Scots, *refers to:*
>'The hawthorn: budding in the glen.'

William Barnes, the nineteenth century Dorset dialect poet, devoted a whole poem to the hawthorn. The May Tree *describes the hawthorn through the seasons, from budding leaves and white blossom to red haws and bare, frost-rimed branches.*

Perhaps the most famous references to hawthorn are in the work of Marcel Proust. In his epic work A La Recherche du Temps Perdu *(Remembrance of Things Past), he describes how:*
'It was in the 'Month of Mary' that I remember having first fallen in love with hawthorns.'

They bedecked the church and altar during the Saturday evening devotions held during May, following the traditional association between the hawthorn and the Virgin.

They were: '… inseparable from the mysteries in whose celebration they participated…'.

He describes their 'serried branches… festoons of leaves…little clusters of buds of a dazzling whiteness.'

Later, Proust describes walking along a path 'throbbing with the fragrance of hawthorn-blossom' and then discovering a pink one:
'…it glowed there, smiling in its fresh pink garments, deliciously demure and Catholic."

The return of the family to Paris that year took place while the hawthorns were still in bloom, and Proust describes his distress at leaving them behind. He vowed

that, as an adult, he would always arrange to 'set off for the country to see the first hawthorn trees in bloom.'
'Wi' May an' all its sheenen flow'rs a-come,
'How sweet vor young wi' young to meet in glee.'
     (William Barnes, Shellbrook)

  'All in this pleasant evening, together comers we,
  'For the summer springs so fresh, green and gay:
  'We'll tell you of a blossom and buds on every tree,
  'Drawing near to the merry month of May.'
       (Swinton May Song)

Common name: hawthorn, may; also many local names such as quickset, whitethorn and holy innocents.

Botanical name: Crataegus monogyna. Also crataegus oxycantha (common name Midland thorn).

Family: Rosaceae.

Growth: slow grower but vigorous coloniser of waste ground; the most frequently used species for hedging enclosing fields.

Lifespan: Average lifespan 100-200 years but can be much more.

Size: height up to 12 metres, girth about one metre.

Flowers: 'may blossom'. Many clusters of single white flowers, each nearly two centimetres across with five petals, five sepals and pink anthers.

Fruit: haw. Round, red, with five woody scales at the top, ripening in October.

Botanical Notes

Leaves: *deciduous. Small, short-stalked, dull green, divided into irregular lobes.*

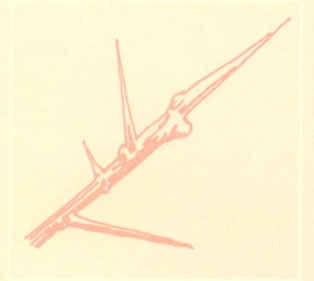

Thorns: *Watch out for prickly stems with thorns which can exceed two centimetres in length.*

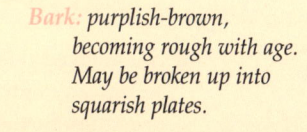

Bark: *purplish-brown, becoming rough with age. May be broken up into squarish plates.*

In the same series

Ash
Box
Cedar of Lebanon
Holly
Monkey Puzzle
Oak
Yew

To be published soon

Beech
Birch
Catalpa
Elm
Hornbeam
Mulberry
Scots Pine
Willow

If you enjoyed this and would like
to buy any of the above titles
or require further information
please contact

SAGE PRESS

PO Box Nº 1, Rye, East Sussex TN31 6HN.
e-mail: sagepress.bm@btinternet.com
Website: sagepress.co.uk